Sweet on my lips

Praise for Sweet On My Lips

Mirabai's spiritual vision and poetic genius shine through these
pages. Verses of wounded pathos and soaring ecstasy are rendered
here as vividly as if they had been spoken yesterday, yet with the
incantatory power of sacred text. Levi's translations, brilliant in
their lucidity, usher the reader directly into the heart of Mira's
rare impassioned devotion.

—Miranda Shaw

The beatutiful poems of Mirabai have been beautifully translated
from the Middle Hindi by Louise Landes Levi, and they should
serve as a fine key to this tantric poet's consciousness.

— Lawrence Ferlinghetti

What makes these translations of Mirabai so remarkable is not so
much this simpatico recognition among poets across time and
space, but that for the first time these poems are rendered in the
context of their original transmissions by one who is herself an
intitiate, tantric practitioner, and acarya of poetics.

—Jacqueline Gens

The West has St. Teresa d'Avila—the East has Mirabai.
Whosoever understands them both understands all there is to
understand.

—Claudio Rugafiori

The power of the book is in its multiple levels of expression: per-
sonal, literary, mystical, intervowen in a manner difficult to
describe. Go back to the poems after you have finished the book.
Are you not a better reader of Mirabai's poetry now? "With tears
I planted the vine of love" sings Mira. "Now that vine is full with
its fruit, Bliss." Sweet on my Lips is such a vine.

— India Radfar

SWEET ON MY LIPS

Radha-Krishna, Kalighat, North India

SWEET ON MY LIPS
the love poems
of
MIRABAI

Louise Landes Levi

coolgrovepress

Landes-Levi, Louise
  Sweet on my lips : the love-poems of Mirabai
  / Louise Landes-Levi.

p. cm.
Includes bibliographical references.
Preassigned LCCN: 96-83816
ISBN 10: 1-887276-04-1
ISBN 13: 978-1-887276-04-7

1. Mirabai, fl. 1516-1546—Criticism and interpretation.
2. Women mystics. 3. Women—India—Social conditions.
4. Love poetry. 7. Bhakti—Poetry. I. Title.

PK2O95.M5Z93 1997   891'.43'12
                                                      QBI96-40340

publisher's acknowledgments
Gratitude to Louise Landes Levi for going the whole nine yards
Candace and Sage-Akash for supporting the reality of small press
the friendly publishers who warned me about small press

SECOND EDITION
[First Edition was published by Coolgrovepress in 1997]

Cool Grove Press
printed in the United States of America

SWEET ON MY LIPS

adhara dhare mrudu bainu

SWEET ON MY LIPS: *the love poems of Mirabai*

CONTENTS

COLOPHON

Some of these translations have been previously published in
Ins and Outs, The Mirror, Resonance, The Path of the Mystic Lover
(Bhaskar Bhattacharya) and *The Water-Mirror* (Louise Landes
Levi). Dutch, Italian and Serbo-Croatian versions of these trans-
lations have appeared, respectively, in Die Kosmos Nieuws Blad,
Zo Maar Wat Verhalen, Dzog-Chen Brief, (transl. B. Mohr),
Prisma (transl. D. Jovanovic), and Mgyur and Dedicato Allo
Scuro (transl. R. Degli-Esposti).

Book and cover design: P. Tej Hazarika and L. L. Levi.
Cover photos: Alex Siedeleki, Krishna murti and dress from the
collection of Yesan Clemente

Photography: Lynn and Jon Weinberger, p.11, 2, 13, 16, 52, 64
Bhaskar Bhattacharya, p. 49, A. Khanna, p.69, B. Raja, p. 74

Author portrait: Ira Cohen, p. 88

Musical composition: Courtesy Professor E. te Nijenhuis

Musical notation: J. R. O'Brien

Line drawings: Vani Dasi Devi. p.3, 5, 68, 75

Publisher's acknowledgements: Louise Landes Levi for her enthu-
siasm and patience in composing this book. Milton & Val
Carrasco and Naresh & Mina Patel, for their generous founding
patronage. Candace for saying I should do a small press. My late
mother Priyam Hazarika for believing in me. Missed and remem-
bered fondly for their love and friendship, Loren Stanley and
Arthur Mandelbaum.

ACKNOWLEDGMENTS

The translator gratefully acknowledges the many teachers, associates and friends who have made this publication possible: Swami Muktananda for his transmission of Sanskrit; Dr. Kumar and Drs. Plukker of the University of Delhi and Amsterdam for their kind and illumined teachings of Mira's Braja Bhasa; Mr. Mukerjee for his introduction to the ambiance of Mira's poetic; Vladislav Klaus for his clarification of certain Sanskrit terms; Jerry Briskin, Bhaskar Bhattacharya and the late Henri Michaux for their insightful readings of the text.

For the American publication: Nancy Simons and Lynn Weinberger for their encouragement in its initial stages; Gene Gawain for his mirror-like generosity, Michael Setter for his assistance with the glossary and the Ali Akbar College of Music for graciously permitting the use of their library, typewriter and working space.

In New York City, in its completion stages: Tej Hazarika, the publisher, for his vision of this work; Steve Taylor, Paul Leake and Sharron Weiner for their hospitality and for opportunities to perform and record this canon, Marlene Hennessy and Arthur Mandelbaum for meticulous editorial work; Barry Simons, Lee Ann Freilich and Joan Milgram for valuable editorial suggestions; and the Jivamukti Yoga Center, especially Sharon Gannon, David Life and Shri Shyam Das, for their support of the resonance and the realization which is at the heart of Mira's bhajan mala.

—landeslevi@gmail.com

The 'Monkey' Temple, Varanasi, North India

PREFACE

According to the great tantric scholar S. Das Gupta (see bibliog. no. 9), the profusion of self-liberating techniques practiced in the formative periods of both Hindu and Buddhist tradition did not emerge specifically from Hindu or Buddhist doctrine, but rather represented and resulted from an indigenous quest for realization— a perennial tradition of transcendence and transformation in the Indian sub-continent.

Mira inherited diverse schools of visionary gift. The school of Krishna bhakti established by Vallabhacharya (1481-1553) was initiatory and continues to the present day. In this teaching aesthetics and enlightenment are paired phenomena, intimately linked both through their object and their method.

In Vallabha's instruction, bhakti yoga or the yoga of devotional love requires both an understanding and an experience of sunyata or emptiness. Nirguna, the emptiness of phenomena, saguna, the totality of phenomena and Narayana (Vishnu or Krishna, see glossary), the birthless deity, are One—as are the poet and the subject of her verse.

The aesthetic formulae are manifestations of enlightened mind and methods of its realization. The subtle body of mantra empowers the verse—raising the poet and the poetic to its own level, in much the way that Krishna draws Radha (or the prakrit, the relative state where we live) into a knowledge of the non-dual state or absolute.

Bhakti requires a deity. For the Vaishnavite, Krishna is the supreme deity, the total personification of godhead. The absolute is ornamented with his qualities, and all qualities emanate his essence. He is worshipped by his devotees as the devata of sunyata or emptiness.

—New York City 1995

My love is only Giradhara Nagara,
Crowned like a peacock, he is my Lord,
Let it be said that I have no honor,
I do not live for family or friend.

Sitting with saints I lost my demeanor,
Tearing my sari, I dressed in a sheet,
I traded my pearls for a garland of flowers,
And with tears I planted the vine of love.

Now that vine is full with its fruit, Bliss.
I pressed on the milk-churn with deep devotion,
Leaving the butter, I drank the butter-milk.

In bhakti I was joyful, in the world I wept,
Mira, the servant, sings Gopala save me.

—Mirabai

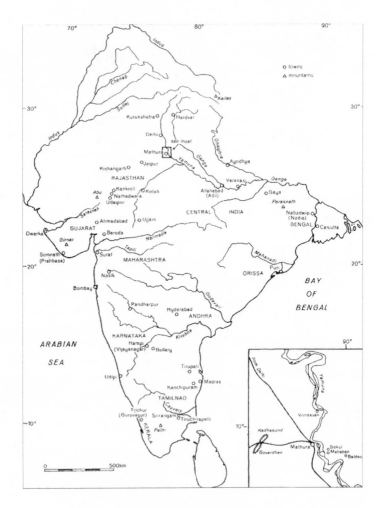

A map of the Indian Subcontinent
(please note that this map does not represent the actual borders
of the contemporay Indian Republic)

INTRODUCTION

Translation is, or can be, an introduction to a state of being (see Daumal's essay, 'The Power of the Word', bibliog. no.11). It is, or can also be, an introduction to a being (as in the translations of specific authors). In the instance of texts which deal with transmission and lineage, the act of translation is a direct path into these essences and the energies they convey.

Mira's deity, the Lord Krishna, was for her both an internal manifestation and a Hindu god. According to some Mira was Radha (incarnate) and thus a goddess. Others simply state that born to manifest the path of realization through devotion, she was an archetypal bhakta whose essence would demonstrate to our confusion the fruit and labor of one-pointed love. Her concentration was on the inner guru. Mirabai rarely refers to Raidas, the adept who introduced her to the tradition, and we receive from her poetry only the barest details of her actual sadhana or spiritual work.

The canons codified by Vallabhacarya, i.e., the *bhavas* or expressive modes of Krishna worship can be found as well within the Tibetan schools of *kriya*, *carya*, and *yoga tantra*. Indeed the word *ishta devata*, or personal deity, translates into Tibetan as *yidam*. Esoteric Christian schools also reveal the mystic union of the adorer and the adored: the poetry of the great Spanish poet, St. John of the Cross, as well as that of John Donne, and more recently, among others in English, Gerard Manley Hopkins. The method of this passion reached an incomparable expression in the work of Jalal al-din Rumi, the great Sufi Master, who longed for and attained the object of his passion, Shams of Tabriz. The song of King Solomon, *The Song of Songs* in the Old Testament, celebrates this same passionate objective.

In this work, I attempted an English translation of a poetry and

Dhrupad singers, Ayodha, North India

a poetic which was developed to convey a teaching whose aesthetic served the purpose of initiation, and whose content was both a description of and an introduction to an objective state. Such poetry, written in what is called in the tantric tradition the *sandhyabhasa* or "twilight language" is particularly difficult to render in our modern Western languages whose etymological roots do not include this level of expression. More than one third of the linguistic content of Mira's songs is in or is directly derived from Sanskrit, the meaning and vibration of which was, for the Indian initiate, a direct reflection of his or her primordial state. And these poems were, and still are sung, intensifying through the unique powers of the Indian musical system, an inherent capacity to transform the consciousness of the listening public.

Introduction

Mira's poems depict the active power of her spiritual work—they are a witness to her realization. Mirabai's poetic and the movement toward a "popular" or vernacular poetry (the commitment of the poet-saints of the period) extended the traditionally inaccessible teachings of the sacred books to those of the non-Brahmanic castes who, as such, had no direct access to the written word (see transl. note, 22).

And the languages of the new genius, Mawari, Naga kari, Awadhi, et. al. liberated from the rigorous formalities of Sanskrit, were rich, fertile and innovative. Mira's songs are exceptionally refined and were appreciated even in her own lifetime by the kings and by her peers, but her lifestyle was that of a yogini. Kings came to her but she, seeking service and not "favor", went to the people and the shrines most associated with the object of her love, Krishna.

In the years which have elapsed since the completion of these translations and their publication, it was my supreme good fortune to meet a master and to profit directly from his physical manifestation. The Mira poems and her one-pointed passion for realization were very much a basis for this further evolution in my life. I hope the reader will be benefitted as well and that my own ego has been left out of this translation to the extent that Mira's secret understanding of devotion can pass through the linguistic transmutations and stylistic devices which were necessary to render the poems.

With infinite gratitude, I dedicate this book to Namkhai Norbu Rinpoche. May the spirit of these poems reach all who treasure the gift of poetry and may beings everywhere benefit from the supreme realization.

Mere to gopala girdhara dusro na hai koi
Jake sura mora mukuta mera pate soi

San Rafael, 1987

3

Mira Bhajan p.20

नींद नहिं आवरी सारी रात ॥
फरवट लेकर सेज टटोलूं (रूँ),
　　　पिया नहीं मोरे साथ ॥ १ ॥
सगली रैन मोघ तड़की बीती,

　　　सोच सोच जिया जात ॥ २ ॥
मीरां के प्रभु गिरधर नागर,
　　　थान मयो परभात ॥ ३ ॥

Mira Bhajan p.21

दरस बिन दूखन लागे नैन ॥
पिया मिलन कां है मन मांही,
　　　कल न पड़त दिन रैन ॥ १ ॥
कबहूँ मिलेंगे प्रीतम प्यारे,
　　　अधर धरे मृदु वेनु ॥ २ ॥
मीरां के प्रभु गिरधर नागर,
　　　बिन देंगे नहिं चेन ॥ ३ ॥

4

Mira Bhajan p.24

पलक न लागें मेरी, स्याम बिन ॥
हरि बिन मथुरा ऐसी लागै,
शशि बिन रैन अंधेरी ॥
पात पात वृन्दावन ढूढ्यो, कुञ्ज-कुञ्ज ब्रजकेरी ।
ऊंचे खड़े मथुरा नगरी, तल नहैं जमना गहरी ॥
मीरां के प्रभु गिरधर नागर,
हरि चरणन की चेरी ॥

Cover, Mira Bhajan Mala, Shyam Khasi Press

THE MIRA BHAJANS

The poems of Mirabai are lyrical representations of her search for and submission to the supreme reality, Krishna, or the inner-self (*atman*). They evolve from a long tradition of Vaishnavite worship but are especially marked by the deep play of love, which both veils and reveals her *sadhana*, or search for self. The poems are *tantric*, the love play is a reflection of her inner state, and the polarities which are involved in the transformation from a relative or subjective to an absolute or objective plane of being.

Mira was an adept of the yogic tradition diffused in the north of medieval India, principally through the great South-Indian Vaishnavite Ramanuja and his disciple Ramananda. Other schools of North Indian *bhakti* (from the Sanskrit root *bhaj*, meaning to share, hence *bhajan*) directly related to this tradition are those of the great poet-saints Chaitanya, Kabir and Tulsidas.

The poems are written in *Braja bhasa*[1], a dialect of the Braja region south of Delhi, the literary language of medieval North India and a specific language of Krishna *bhakti* . The language is etymologically linked to scholarly Sanskrit and its dialects, especially *Aparabhramsa* (seventh-twelfth century A.D.) but unlike Sanskrit, whose laws of composition and grammar were regarded as fixed expressions of sacred power, the dialects emerged from social and linguistic changes which created new language forms and the possibility for a free interplay between the poet, the language and the deity or *ishta devata*.

The form of the poems or *padas* derive from an earlier Sanskrit structure, the *caryaapada*, developed by the *siddha*

7

poets and later refined and made accessible to the Vaishnavite tradition by the East Indian poets (twelfth-fourteenth century A.D.) Jayadeva, Chandidasa and Vidyapati. These *padas* are characterized by the author's signature in the second-to-last line and by the introductory *teka* or statement from which the thematic aspect of the poem develops.

Each *pada* was, in addition, written for a specific *raga* (melodic mode) and *tala* (rhythmic mode), and included within its composition a specific *rasa*[2] (aesthetic mode), a specific *bhava* (or expressive mode), a specific meter and a specific delineation with regard to the time of day and to the exact season. The majority of the *padas* describe a state of separation before union, or the longing for divine absorption. Technically, the *rasa* is *sringara*—*the* mode of spiritual intoxication, represented through the parable of erotic sensibility in the form of *vipralabdha*, or separation.

According to Vallabhacarya, the great Krishna *bhakta* and exponent of Vedanta in Braj, the love of Lord Krishna was to be expressed through four essential modes: 1) service or *dasya bhava*, 2) friendship or *sakya bhava*, 3) parental love or *vatsalya bhava* and 4) marriage or *madhurya bhava*. Mira most frequently addresses Krishna as his servant or wife; the quality and the power of her devotion is not linked to subjective emotion or sentiment. It is rather a matrix of transubstantiation, a transcendent love, a yoga through which the mutual relation of *guru* and *sisya* (teacher and student) fulfills itself, and through which, in the tantric tradition, Mira merges into the guru or inner self.[3]

Mira was born in approximately 1498 A.D. in Merta, Rajasthan. Raised as a princess, chosen by the Rajput rulers to be the first Hindu queen of medieval North India, her inner life was completely concentrated on Lord Krishna. Legend asserts that the wandering and low-

The Mira Bhajans

The Lake Palace, Udaipur, North India.

caste ascetic Raidas, a disciple of Ramananda, presented her with a statue of Krishna. She is said to have received an immediate spiritual transmission from the statue or murti which she thenceforth, from the age of three or four, worshipped as the divinity.

Married at the age of eighteen to Bhoraj, the heir-apparent to the Rajput throne, she was widowed several years later and consequently never ruled the region. Persecuted by her in-laws for her religious practices and her inadvertent political affiliations, her devotion to Lord Krishna and the intensity of her sadhana were unaffected. Miraculous occurrences, attributed to divine intervention, saved her from assassination on several occasions.

In 1531 she definitively left the Rajput court and the controversies which surrounded her. After a brief stay in Chittor, where her uncle had his residence, she undertook a series of peregrinations, traveling through the regions of Rajasthan, Gujarat, and Braja. She sought refuge in the temples of Mathura on the banks of the Yamuna, in Uttar Pradesh and Dwarka, in Saurashtra. These cities were closely associated with the legends of Krishna and with the bhakti. they inspired. A trained musician, she sang her compositions to the accompaniment of her vina, while a female companion or servant, Leela or Lalita, is said to have faithfully recorded the padas in written form.[4]

Refused a darshan (or meeting) with a well-known pandit, Jiva Gosain, because she was a woman,[5] she is reputed to have said, "In the region of Braja, all souls are female with respect to Krishna, Vasudeva, the absolute." Other legends describe her meeting with the Mogul emperor Akbar,[6] his brilliant musician Tansen and the poet Tulsidas, but there are historic controversies regarding the details. It is certain, however, that although she established no school or lineage, she was a legendary figure in the medieval North, known for her courage, her powers and the immediate passion of her devotional singing.

In response to a Brahminic emissary sent, circa 1550 from Udaipur to recall her to the Rajput Court, Mira begged an evening's respite in the Ranchorji Temple of Dwarka. In the morning, she had disappeared, leaving behind, it is said, only her sari, draped across the Krishna *murti*.

Mira wrote over four hundred poems, of which one hun-

The Yamuna ghats, Mathura, North India

dred and five form a core positively ascribed to her. The poems reveal the deepening levels of her love, at first describing the separation from the court and the difficulties she encountered, and later, her complete absorbtion in the presence of Lord Krishna and her relationship to him. The allegorical states of separation and union clearly refer to levels of her *sadhana* (or spiritual work), as the references to sleep and wakefulness denote the stages of awareness experienced in her search for the absolute level of consciousness.

—Paris 1977

NOTES:

1. Mira's Braja is not a pure form of the language as it is infused with forms from both Rajasthani and Gujarati, but, essentially, it is the Braja dialect. For this reason, along with Mira's clear affinity to the *bhakti* poets of Braja, she is classified with the poets of that region.

2. "The sense of *rasa* is a pleasure which has no relation to any particular ego. The aesthetic state of consciousness does not insert itself into the texture of everyday life, but is seen and lived in complete independence of any individual interest. This state implies the elimination of any measure of time and space (time and space belonging to discursive thought) and, by implication, the limited knowing subject who is conditioned by these, but who during the aesthetic experience, raises himself, momentarily, above the stream of his practical life, *samsara*. Aesthetic experience makes a definite break with *samsara*, which is conditioned by the laws of cause and effect." (Abhinavagupta-Gnoli, see bibliog. no. 14.)

3. According to the Hindu *tantric* teaching, the guru or "self" resides in the seventh and highest *chakra*, the *saharasrara*. The love-play which is delineated in the poetry of Mira can be seen as an expression of the yogic process whereby the *shakti* or conscious energy, dormant in the *kundalini*, awakes, approaches and finally unites with the lord or guru in the *sahasrara*. (See Woodroffe, bibliog. no. 49 & glossary, Terms 4 & 7)

4. Unfortunately, the original manuscripts of the *padas*, said to have been transcribed by her companion Lalita, were lost when the Ranchorji Temple was looted in an invasion in the 17th Century.

11

5. The only female in an otherwise male devotional community, Mira was initially isolated and ostracized in her quest. Later, however, her 'female-ness' was acknowledged as a special attribute in the *sadhana* (of Krishna *bhakti*), Radha *bhava*, which permitted her actual embrace of Krishna, which even Chaitanya, it was implied, could not experience (and which her peers had initially rejected as *anugata-sadhana*). Simply speaking, Mira came to be accepted as a *gopi*, a cowherd companion and lover of Krishna, or even as an incarnation of Radha, the principal consort of the youthful god, by the very community which had at first rejected her.

6. The Muslim invasions of North India (*circa.* eighth-thirteenth century A.D.) destroyed much of the Buddhist and Hindu world. They did introduce, however, a passionate form of mystical expression, in which the relation to God or the absolute was seen and depicted as a personal one: the lover, as the disciple (or individual soul) and the loved-one as the totality of love, the guru, or as in Mira's poetic, the deity, Krishna.

Akbar, the great Mogul emperor of the sixteenth century was renowned for his tolerance toward both Hindu and Buddhist communities. He summoned to his court the country's most brilliant scholars and artists, irrespective of their religious affiliations. Together with these "Nine Jewels," as they were called, he established an unprecedented wave of artistic development and intellectual innovation in medieval North India. The legend of the meeting between Akbar and Mira cannot be proven historically, but as it is part of her hagiography, it is included here.

Temple Ruin, Kashmir, North India

SWEET ON MY LIPS
the love poems
of
MIRABAI

TRANSLATED
BY
LOUISE LANDES LEVI

Banyan tree, temple courtyard, South India

nityam suddham nirabhasam
nirakaram niramjanam
nityabodham cidanandam
gurum brahma mamamyaham

—Guru Gita, 90.

"I am the self in the inner-most
heart of all, I am their
beginning, middle and end.

The science of soul among sciences,
I am the speech of letters,
I am A."

—Krishna, *Bhagavad Gita*

"Those who contemplate on this subtle
eternal and ancient deity, of the
luster of the pure blue sky,

They do not attach any importance
to learning, sacrifices,
gifts or severe penance."

—Ramanuja

I sing the powers of Govinda,[1]

The king, displeased,
    His kingdom, unmoving,
Hari,[2] displeased,
    There's no escape,

The king sent poison
    in a cup,
        I tasted nectar,
He sent a black snake
    in a basket,
        I received a saligram[3]

Mira is in love with
    Her consort
      Sanvaliya.[4]

Black-one[5]
    Come
       to my home,

Yellowed
    as an autumn leaf,
      I long for
        thought
          of you,

Swami,[6] Mira's lord,
    Meet me,
      Save my
       honor.

Sleepless, sleepless,
      I twist on my bed,
            My beloved is not
                  with me,

The night tormented,
      My thoughts
            dark,

O Lord of Mira, giradhara,[7]
      Another dawn has
            come.

I can not see you,
   My eyes burn,
     My mind is taken
       by
        you,

Day and night,
   Without patience,
     When will you meet me,
    Lord,

The words, sweet
   on my lips,
    Girdhara

Without seeing you,
   I can not see.

I've lost myself
   Rama[8]
    I'm waiting for
     a word from
    you,

I'm restless and
    pale.

Did you fall in love
   with a friend
   of mine,
Is she more beloved
   than I?

Please show yourself,
   I'll forgive all
   your faults,

Once in your
   shelter,
    Kind-one.

My breath, my breath,
   Hari,
      My shelter, Hari,

I saw the illusion,
   I saw the
      Three-Worlds[9]

You alone can please,

Mira says,
   I'm yours,
      Don't forget.

Without the Dark-one,
    I can not sleep.

Without Hari,
    Mathura[10] is a night
        without a moon,

I look in the leaves of
    Brindavana,[11]
        In the brush of
        Braja,[12]

Like water flowing
    beneath
        Mathura,

Dark-one,
    I bow to your
        Lotus-feet.[13]

Friend,[14] in Braja, I saw
   something strange,

  A Gujari[15] sold curds,
    then she met with Nandana,[16]
     and forgetting herself,

   cried, "Who will buy
    Shyama,
     the beloved?"

He has struck Brindavana
   with his Love,

Mira's Lord whose eyes
   are filled with
    love.

I saw the clouds and cried, Shyama,
   I saw the clouds and cried,

   They were black and yellow,
      and round with rain,
   I stood outside waiting while
      the earth grew green,

   O Love, you live in a foreign land,
      but my love for you
         is unchanging,

      my Lord,
         the indestructible.
         Hari.

The separated sleepless,
    when the world sleeps, friend,
        one strings pearls in her palace,
            another threads tears.

    The night has passed
        counting the stars,

    Mira waits for
        the hour-of-pleasure,
            when the Dark-one will
                take away her pain.

O Friend, I couldn't sleep,
  I spent the night
    in search of him,

    You tried to advise me,
      I couldn't obey,

  Restless, restless,
    who destined my life,

    in each limb pain,
      and on my lips,
        the cry, Beloved,

  No one hears my call,
    like the Cataka[17] cries
      to the cloud,
        like the fish remembers
          the sea,

    Mira is impatient,
      she is separated,
        she is senseless
          with Love.

I'm longing to meet
   with
     Shyama,
  but he's gone,
    He's settled in
      Dwarka,[18]

On the mango
   the crow sings
     sorrowfully,

but the people
   are laughing
     at me,

Disturbed, I wander
   here,
     there,

O giradhara, I serve
   your
     Lotus-feet.

I slept for a moment,
　　the Beloved appeared,
　　　　when I rose to greet him,
　　　　　he was
　　　　　　gone,

　　Some lose him
　　　sleeping,
　　　　I lost him
　　　　　awake,

　　Mira's lord, giradhara,
　　　brings happiness to
　　　　the
　　　　　home.

Drink the nectar, Rama,
  drink the nectar of
    the name[19],

    Avoid evil, sit with saints,
      listen to the legend
        of
          Hari,

    Passion, pride, greed, ego,
      Out-of-mind,

    Mira is dyed the color
        of
          Lord
            Hari.

Rana,[20] I go to giradhara,
I'm lost in the love
for giradhara,

Our marriage is old,
Our marriage is from
the past,

To me it doesn't matter,
that we were married
in a dream,

Mother, Dinnatha,[21]
wed me, in my
dream.

How can I write to Hari?

My pen, full, my heart,
  frail.
    In my mind,
      the words,
        silenced.
      In my eyes,
        tears,

If I can not write a
  letter,

How shall I touch
  his lotus-feet?

Mira asks giradhara
  to take away her
    pain.

I stood on the path,
    no one saw my pain,

    A guru passed,
      he gave me medicine,

        every pore found
          peace,

    Ask the Veda,[22]
      ask the Purana,[23]

    The only doctor
      is a
        Sadguru,[24]

    Mira's lord is giradhara,

    His permanent residence,
    The house
       of
        bliss.

The Dark-one,

    like a moon
       grown pale,

    went to Madhuban,[25]
       became
         Madhubani,

Left us lost
    in
       love's net.

O giradhara,

Did your affection
    wane?*

To love a yogi is sorrow's root,

He seems to be friendly,
    he charms, he forgets,

He plucks out his loves
    like jasmine,

Mira says, giradhara,

You pierce the heart
    with pain.*

   I
looked for the Dark-one,

   I
found his image
   in my heart,

   I
stood in his court,
   my life in his hands,
     only his medicine healed,

  Mira sold to giradhara,
   the world calls her
    wayward.

Kind-one, hear my complaint,
I'm floating on a cosmic sea,
I've gone the whole way,

I've no friend in this world,
my only friend is
Radhubarji.[26]

Mother, father, family, forsaken,
they're on the outside,

Mira's Lord, Listen,
I've surrendered to
your
Lotus-Feet.

O Friend, I'm maddened with
   love,
       I can't sleep on a bed
         of nails,
       when the bed of love
        is near,

   Which is the way
       to
         union?

   Only the wounded know
      the wound,

   Only the jeweler knows
      the jewel,

   In pain, I wander from
      wood
        to
          wood,

   In search of the doctor
      to heal me,
       Sanvaliya.

Yogi, I'm your slave
don't leave,
show me
Love's path,

Ignite
the
pyre,

burn
the
branch,

Press my ash,
to your palms,
your pores.

Mira says,
Yogi,
make two flames

One.

My beloved came,
  I watched the road,
    and I, the solitary,
      attained Him,

I decorated the plate
    for puja,[27]
I gave my jewels
    to Him,

And finally,
    He sent messages,
    He came,

Bliss adorns me,
    Hari is a sea
      of love,

My eyes are linked
    to his,
      in Love,

Mira, a sea of bliss,
    admits
      the Dark-one.

Indian miniature, 17th Century

NOTES TO THE MIRABAI TRANSLATIONS

1. **Govinda**: An epithet for Krishna, from the Sanskrit go meaning cowherd. It can also be understood as "he-who-knows-the-*Veda*".

2. **Hari**: A name for Shiva, also a particular deity consisting of Vishnu and Siva joined from the Sanskrit, *hri*, to lift, to steal, to steal from the heart, *hrim*, seed syllable of the heart.

3. **Saligrama** or s**aligram**: A cone-shaped spiral fossil (ammonite), found in the Himalayas and believed to be a self-willed manifestation of a deity, especially of Vishnu.

4. **Sanvaliya**: An epithet of Krishna, from the Sanskrit, meaning "he-who unites".

5. **Black-one or dark-one**: In the Sanskrit, *Shyama*, meaning dark blue one, an epithet for Krishna.

6. **Swami**: A title of a spiritual teacher, indicating respect and generally given to a renunciate who has taken specific vows.

7. **giradhara**: From the Sanskrit, *gir*, meaning mountain, and *dhara*, to hold. Referring to one of Krishna's exploits in which, with one finger, he held up the sacred mountain in Braj, Mount Govardhan for seven days and stood beneath it, in order to protect his worshippers from a wrathful flood sent by Indra.

8. **Rama**: The seventh incarnation of Vishnu, the all-pervading. According to Vaishnavite sources, Krishna was the eighth, Lord Buddha the ninth, and Kalki the tenth and last incarnation is yet to come. From the Sanskrit, *ram*, to rejoice, also *ram*, seed syllable of the fire element. (See glossary Vishnu)

9. **Three Worlds**: In the Sanskrit, *tri-loka*, meaning earth, heaven and hell. The indication is that Krishna is beyond our conceptual processes, beyond that which we can conceive with our minds. (Also a reference to the *turiya*, the state beyond the other three of waking, sleeping and dreamless sleep.)

10-12. **Mathura, Brindaban and Braja**: Mathura and Brindaban, the cities principally associated with the childhood and youth of Krishna, are located on the banks of the sacred River Yamuna to the southeast of Delhi. Braja

43

is to the West of Mathura. All three cities are still in existence and it is believed that Krishna's ecstatic dance with the *gopi*, the *ras-lila*, is still enacted in the Shiva Kunj, a park in Brindaban (see Map, p.xvi and glossary-*Rasa*).

13. **Lotus-feet**: In the Sanskrit *kamala charana*. According to the Hindu tantra, the guru's feet contain his shakti, or energy, so that obeisance to them is a sign of respect as well as a method to obtain his accumulated potency.

14. **Friend**: In the Sanskrit, *sakhi*, a female confident or companion. Haridas saw himself as the incarnation of Lila or Lalita, the *sakhi* or confidante of Mira. He wrote, "Mira worshipped Lord Giradhara, discarding laws of family and decorum. This same Mira became world famous for her devotion. When Lalitaji (incarnate as Haridas) met her in Brindaban, she was shown round all the ancient dalliance spots by him" (trans. B. Behari).The *sakhi* did not long for union with Krishna, but merely to witness the *lila* (or divine play) between Radha and Krishna.

15. **Gujari**: A woman from the region of Gujarat, southwest of Delhi and north of Bombay.

16 **Nandana**: Literally, the son of Nanda, Krishna's adopted father, according to the tradition his real father was Vasudeva; also joy (in Sanskrit), hence the product or the fruit of joy itself.

17. **Cataka**: A mythic bird who mates only during the rainy season and who only drinks water which has not yet touched the earth.

18. **Dwarka**, or **Dvaraka**: Located in Saurashtra, a region in the northwest of India, this city, still in existence, was the site from which Krishna, in his adult years, ruled together with his consort Rukmini. Dwarka is considered one of the seven sacred cities of India, a mere visit to which, according to the tradition, confers liberation. The others are Mathura, Ayodhya, Maya or Haridwar, Kasi, Kanchi, and Avantika or Ujain (see Map, p.xvi).

19. **Name**: In the Sanskrit nama. In the tradition, the name of something is its subtle form as well so that recitation of the name of a deity is a subtle form of unification with that deity.

44

20. **Rana**: Literally, king, most probably Rana Ratansingh, the father of Mira, but perhaps Maharana Pratap, the father of Mira's deceased husband, Bhoraj.

21. **Dinnatha**: An epithet for Krishna, from the Sanskrit *din*, meaning poor, and natha, lord, master or protector; hence "protector of the poor."

22. **Veda**: From the Sanskrit vid, meaning knowledge. According to the Hindu tradition, the four *Veda*—the *Rig, Yajur, Soma* and *Atharva*, have "existed in their perfection since the beginning of time." Transmitted orally, even before the invention of the Sanskrit alphabet, they were codified in our age by the sage Vyasa. A collection of sacred verse and ritualistic formula, their content (*sruti*) was accessible only to those of Brahmanic initiation, a mandate which applied as well to the *Brahmanas* and the *Upanishads* (see also glossary, Vedanta).

23. **Purana**: Literally, "Ancient Stories," sixth-sixteenth century A.D., a compendium of ancient legends and religious instruction. There are 18 principal *puranas*. The ninth or tenth, the *Bhagavata Purana*, is the one associated with Lord Krishna. Each *purana* possesses *lakshana* or marks which distinguish its contents; there are six *purana* each for Shiva, Brahma and Vishnu. Part of the *smrita* or non-vedic literature, their study was not limited to the sacerdotal castes.

24. **Sadguru**: From the Sanskrit *sat*, meaning true, and *guru*, meaning master; hence, a true master or master of the truth. In the tradition, the *sadguru* was not only realized, he had the inherent capacity to bring others to this state. Bankey Behari states that, according to Mira herself, "The supernatural *swarup* (form) of the *sadguru* was (due to the fact) that the Gurus who descend from heaven are embodiments of grace. They are not men who ascend to heaven, by effort and *sadhana*, and hence their supernatural power. Their body is not a karmic creation". (Behari, bibliog. no. 4)

25. **Madhuban**: From the Sanskrit *madhu*, meaning honey, and *ban*, meaning forest; hence honey forest, here a symbol for erotic intoxication, and *Madhubani*, an inhabitant of that region. Also a reference to an actual city, one of the twelve vaha in the vicinity of Mathura.

26. **Raghubarji**: An epithet for Rama, "*Rama-Rajya*," the blameless and perfect Rama, Jewel of the Solar Kings. The "Solar Dynasty" is said to have originated with Raghu, a descendant of the semi-divine King Manu Vaivasvata, who was the hereditary priest to the rulers of Ayodhya, Rishi of the seventh mandala of the *Rig Veda* and *Manu* or "original man" of

the present age (according to the *Vedas*, each *yuga*, or age, would have a *Manu* who presides over its destiny). Rama is considered to be sixty-fifth in the lineage, but according to the *Matsya Purana*, Siddharta Gautama, the Buddha, was twenty fifth in the same solar line.

27. **Puja**: From the Sanskrit *pu*, meaning, to worship, to adore, to revere the Guru, in the Indian tradition, "formal worship of or offering to the teacher in his actual or imagined form." According to Namkhai Norbu, to make an offering (*puja*) means "to find ourselves in a state of integration; therefore we speak of the infinite offerings for we understand that all of these offerings are actually the qualifications of our primordial state" (transl. John Reynolds).

Indian miniature, Pahari School, 17th century

TRANSLATOR'S NOTE I

A transliteration of the first poem in this selection is transcribed below. The notation follows standard *devanagari* usage, except that no syllable in Braja ends on a non-nasalized consonant; each word ends with a vowel or with "a", resulting in the melodious flow of the Braja poem. The Braja poets employed various meters, *pada, caupadi, doha, yoga*, etc. These were derived from Sanskrit rhetoric usage in which all aspects of composition were considered to be forms of the deity.

MAIN GOVINDA GUNA GANA
(see p. 18: I sing the powers of Govinda)

Main govinda guna gana
Raja ruthe nagari nakhai
Hari ruthajna kahana jana
Rana bhejya jahara piyala
Imarita kara pijana
Ibiya main bhejya ja bhajangama
Saligrama kara jana
Mirato aba prema dibani
Sanvaliya vara pani

The Mira poems were approached on both an interior and a linguistic plane in order to render these translations. The selection represents a nine year period of research, travel and experience. Seeking direct expression, translator experimented with many poetic styles, finally setting the padas in forms derived from study and from a personal sense of tradition and transformation. Braja is a

47

medieval language whose linguistic and devotional roots have no correspondence in English. Even when parallel grammatical or stylistic construction was possible, it was not possible to transform the sensibility and immediacy of Mira's search into a contemporary English expression without interpretive, grammatical and poetic innovation.

The Braja poetic surface is, in itself, a power. In its plenitude it mirrors Mira's divine object. The precise music of the Braja poem, the sensitivity of its one and two syllable words, the beautiful *tatsam* (Sanskrit) usage and the subtle relation between the construction of the language and its content have been sacrificed in translation. The translator hopes that despite the limitations of this selection, the poems will provide a true reflection of the tradition, the inspiration of its adepts and the depth of their attainment.

Mira's poetry is addressed to consciousness, as is the entire tradition of aesthetic representation in the period which preceded the British colonization of India. In each of their details, these poems serve the process of self-attainment. No aspect of the tradition operates independently from this criterion, in which both the poem and poet are aspects of Vishnu in his dynamic form. A literary translation can only suggest the potency with which this principle is realized in these seemingly simple lyrics, composed by a princess-poet-saint seized with a divine vision.

—Paris 1977

[The translator especially acknowledges the work of Bankey Behari and Ussa Nilsson whose translations of Mirabai have been printed in India (see Bibliography). Several poems from the work of Ussa Nilsson have been transliterated for this collection. These poems are indicated with an asterisk (*).]

Translator's note II

Bahurupi: Radha and Krishna, at a bus stop in
Bolpur, Bengal, Eastern India

My work with Sanskrit texts and related expression have their root in a personal experience of the *Devanagari* alphabet which revealed to me that this language is a part of a transmission which is "beyond". I literally learned the *Devanagari* alphabet from a dog; there was no learning in the conventional (Cartesian) sense. There was no learner, instead there was a process whereby the light energy of the letters and my mind conjoined to produce instantaneous learning. Such an experience is a gift. It opened a gate to the fire of Sanskrit recitation and to a very deep inspiration to work with texts written in *Devanagari*.

I was very fortunate to meet a unique master of *Ati yoga* who became my teacher, mentor and friend. This master could communicate to and awaken my state. As he healed the wounds of my vital and subtle fields, he gave me more and more space to discover my capacities and to transcend my limitations. For eight years, no word of Sanskrit was mentioned. Then suddenly, in Venice, in the spring of this year, he said, "Louise", and called me to the room where he was sitting. An Italian astrologer had brought a text in

49

Devanagari and calmly my teacher said, "Read this and tell me what it is". And repeatedly, after this (although never before), he would ask me to transliterate and even help me to discern the words or text himself.

I feel this book is the task for which he was preparing me, as it required a return to a bygone period, to its emotional involvements, and to its unfinished psychological, aesthetic and spiritual aspects.

I hope the reader will excuse any errors of transcription or translation and profit, as I have, from the passionate love of Mira and the realization which was the cause and the fruit of that love.

—San Rafael, 1987

From top to bottom: *Ajna-chakra*, with the letters *Ha* and *Ka*, between the eyebrows the Visuddha *cakra*, with the 16 vowels of the Sanskrit alphabet at the throat, and the Anahata *cakra*, with the 12 sanskrit consonants *ka* to *tha*, at the heart (See glossary page 86)

Sun Goddess, Konarak, North East India

APPENDIX 1

You dominate one state,
Another is dominated by Bhavani.
Pregnant with all of material creation,
Ultimately there is no difference
Between Devi, the three worlds and You.
—Utpaladeva
Hymn to Shiva, 900 A.D (Kashmir)

THE GODDESS

At a recent retreat in Cazadero, Northern California, I request-
ed that my teacher, the *Ati yoga* master Namkhai Norbu, reveal to
me the nature of the *dakini* in the Tibetan tradition. Indicating by
his response that this was to be known empirically, rather than by
his revelation, he asked that I write (for the Dzog-Chen Newsletter)
a description of the female principle in the Sanskrit tradition. I
hereby fulfill his noble request.

According to the Vedic texts, the goddess is recognized in her
three forms as *para*, *sthula* and *suka*. These are each considered to be
aspects of her non-dual nature and in no way are a reflection of an
exclusively female entity. In her *para* form, she is considered to be
"beyond"; beyond name and form (*nama* and *rupa*), beyond concep-
tualization, the absolute non-dual whole. In her *sthula* form, she
manifests as *mantra*, recitation of which is both a means of address-
ing (exoterically) and unifying (esoterically) with her. In her *suka*
form, she is revered as the totality of existence, and as such, all that
lives, male, female, organic, inorganic, audible, inaudible, visible
and invisible substance.

53

Mirabai, the great 16th Century *bhakta* (or devotee) who achieved realization through her one-pointed devotion to Lord Krishna, said, when refused entrance to a temple in Brindavan because she was female, "We are all female (*prakrit*) with regard to Krishna Vasudeva, the absolute" and was admitted to the temple. (See p. 9 & p.12 note 5 of this book for details.)

The term *devi*, in the Sanskrit tradition, (literally, "goddess," etymologically the female form of *deva*, meaning, "light," among other secondary significations) does not imply a dominance of the female, in itself, or that the goddess is a female. The goddess was and is a means, in the tradition, of addressing the absolute in its manifest and non-manifest forms.

Accordingly, the worship of the *devi* was not considered to be in opposition to or in any essential way different from the worship of the deva. Both the *devi* and the *deva* were, rather, *ishta devatas* or personal deities, concentration upon which led the practitioner to realization.

In the Indian tradition, *devi* worship concentrated on Paravati, Lakshmi, Saraswati et al., the peaceful manifestations; and Durga, Kali, Bhairavi et al., the wrathful manifestations; and these were worshipped by male and female practitioners alike. The *ishta devati* were not seen as exclusively female entities; rather they were considered as "matrix" of the divine principle, itself above the dualism which binds us to samsara and the pain of our individualizing egos

According to my limited understanding, in her many manifestations the *devi* was a means to obtain the awakened state. Rather than being a personification, significant only when in the service of our relative understanding, she was a gate, in the tradition, a method, a cosmic power with which to integrate and through which to obtain the state of the unconditioned mind.

—San Rafael, 1987.
[Repr. from the Dzog-Chen Newsletter, Point Reyes, CA, 1987.]

Bhairavi

APPENDIX II

ON
THE SACRED WORD,
POETRY
AND THE ART OF TRANSLATION

I had a longing to go to India for as long as I can remember. As a child, every school report had to be on India, or Japan. Later in life, a parapsychologist, who was also, in some way, my first teacher[1] told me, "You were always Indian or Japanese. This is your first time here. It would be easy for you to learn Sanskrit or Japanese". I thought, no wonder I've always been so slow. No wonder I could never learn Western table manners as a child. No wonder I don't understand the rhythms of Western courtship. I had already noted my capacity to learn both Devanagari and Japanese characters nearly on sight.

Ali Akbar Khan's Indian music school opened in Berkeley in 1968. At first too shy to even apply, I later won a scholarship to study sarangi. I had participated, with other Bay Area artists, in the formation of Daniel Moore's Floating Lotus Magic Opera Company, our version of Tibetan opera, culminating with a grand recitation of the mantra OM AH HUNG VAJRA GURU PADMA SIDDHI HUNG, which we had learned from a record (Danielou, A. (Ed)., *Music of Tibet, Unesco Ser., Vol. l*).

I played Tibetan horn and flute in this opera and, on the basis of these performances, won a scholarship. In my heart, however, I felt my own music was not very developed. My flute improvisations did not compare, for example, to the tradition of classical flute repertory including the sonatas of J.S. Bach which I had studied, nor did I have as deep an experience when playing. I decided to go to India to study music, prompted by my teacher's attentions, which both alienated and appealed to me, and which later provided the cause or need for purification, to which I dedicated myself by translating into English, over a period of seven years, René Daumal's *RASA. Essays on Indian Aesthetics and Selected Sanskrit Studies*, published ten years after I had left India, fragile and broken in the wake of my experiences there.

These experiences, however, were intricate and deep. Swami Muktananda was not well known in the West at the time except to a small group in New York City. He gave darshan or spiritual audience in Bombay to large groups of Indians and some Westerners. I attended several such gatherings, always attired in Indian dress. At one such meeting, I remember seeing Da Free (before he was Da Free John); at another, Baba Ram Das.

One afternoon, as I returned from such a satsang to my small hut, just outside of Bombay in a village called Juhu, I noticed a strange phenomenon. As I walked through the market place, all the small animals followed me. They formed a veritable line of pigs, ducks, geese, dogs, et al. Since I had tried to keep a low profile, to be the French teacher of the local school and not the 'local hippie', I was dismayed. The animals were 'blowing my cool'. So I tried to steer them away. I turned and said, "Please go away". I was actually more concerned with the social effects of being followed by the creatures than the cause of the parade.

I passed the temple courtyard, site of so many beautiful plays and recitations, and headed for my little hut, located on the estate of Sumati Muragi, a wealthy shipping magnate known for her devotion to both Krishna and Gandhi. Ms. Muragi's husband was a being, who, dressed as a woman, it was whispered, worshipped Krishna day and night in a separate building which was both a temple and a home for him.[2]

As I turned down the path through their property, a large black dog, previously a tranquil animal, leaped up and seriously tore into the flesh of my leg. I was rushed to the hospital to receive painful rabies injections. The hospital needle was a foot long, or more, and the injection was administered, without anesthetics, directly into the stomach. I later learned that a large black dog is a symbol of Shiva, the God of destruction, in Indian mythology.

The compound was ablaze with the news, "Louise *taklif hai*." "Louise is in trouble." Mrs. Moraji came to my hut, previously reserved for wandering or visiting sadhus, and invited me to stay, instead, in her home, a beautiful Indian villa, the first floor of which was also a museum. She tucked me into a large wooden bed on the upstairs verandah, just next to a bed, she said, in which Gandhi had slept. He had in fact given the famous Salt Address from her balcony.

The next morning I awoke with my mind in a special state. My leg, after a doctor's visit the previous afternoon, was in traction, and I could not move at all. But I knew that on that day I could learn Sanskrit. In that one day I learned to read, write, and pronounce the letters of the Sanskrit alphabet. It was as if my mind was a lens of light and every letter of the alphabet got photographed onto but was also previously imprinted on that lens. In the Bhagavad Gita, Krishna says "The science of Soul, among sciences, I am the speech of letters. I am A."

After this, I recovered from the dog bite, easily learned Hindi and often went to Baba Muktananda's ashram. I was not completely attracted to him. I was very young and actually afraid of him. I preferred Baba Nityananda, his dead guru, and my friend Denise de Casabianca, the editor of Godard's controversial film, The Nun, who was now living at the ashram. The first day I went to Ganesh Puri, six other Westerners also went there. We were the first group of Westerners to arrive.

Muktananda always directed me to the quarters of the Indian

Appendix II: On word, poetry and the art of translation

women and I slept on the floor with them, never in the dormitories. I was the first Westerner in Ganesh Puri to read Sanskrit perfectly. Of course, I did not know what I was reading but reading Sanskrit was like reading music for me.

I noticed that various, often very bizarre, beings would come to the ashram and sing in Sanskrit for hours. I listened to these recitations with rapt attention. The prayers built up a fiery heat. It sometimes seemed as if I could see the flames which the Sanskrit letters were creating. I had read in Roger Shattuck's introduction to René Daumal's Mount Analogue (City Lights Press) that he, Daumal, had a similar perception and wrote to my cousin, in Paris, to send Daumal's studies on India, in particular, Bharata, to me.

I studied these and tried to apply Daumal's theory of translation to my own work. I worked on and off, for the next ten years, on the poetry of Mirabai. When in Paris, in 1977, I started to formulate an initial manuscript, I realized that I had been to nearly every one of her pilgrimage sites, without even knowing it when I was in India, and for the most part, only to these sites.

I travelled to Udaipur, the medieval seat of the Rajput court, where Mira lived in the early years of her marriage, with my first music teacher, whose family was from that city . The train ride there was very magical. I felt I was going to a place I already knew and, once there, of course, I had some very unusual experiences.

Waking at dawn, in a stable turned motel, I entered the city, not even waiting for the arrival of my music teacher with whom I had an appointment. My feet seemed to know the streets already. I 'flew' through the city. The people asked, "Are you a bride?" until I arrived at the lake, in the middle of which is the Palace of Udaipur (see p.9). I felt I had tried to describe that scene many times in my own poetry.

Later, with my teacher, I went to the 'Mira' temple, outside Udaipur. It was Holi, a sacred day (and night) for the Hindus, when

59

normal conventions are broken and people, in a ritual related to the Spring harvest, splatter colored dye on each other. The evening festivities were indescribably beautiful. My own teacher, normally a reserved, self-conscious person, raised his arms to the skies and, in the courtyard of the temple, danced in circles to the music.

I first heard the word Mathura at an Indian train station and knew I had to go there. A year later, I was in the Mathura Hotel, on the banks of the Yamuna, with a friend who was also a student of music. We listened to Sanskrit *slokas* recited by the local brahmins in the courtyard across the street, drank bhang on the street with them and embarked on a rare boating party. Dhrupad music, sung in Braja, by local musicians filtered across the waters of the Yamuna River on a serene night that belonged to hagiography.

We went, by ricksaw, through the forest to the nearby village of Brindavan (see Map, p. xvi) and were the only Westerners at a performance of the *raslila*, all others in the 'audience' being sadhus with the exception of an orphan child, strangely drawn to us. All the dancers, including those enacting the roles of Radha and the gopis, were young boys, twelve or thirteen years old. A local, self-appointed guide led us to the Siva Kunj, a barren park, where, it is said, this same raslila, is enacted, for 'real', nightly by Krishna and the gopis. Mortal eyes must not behold the spectacle, indeed those, including the monkeys, who remain in the park after sunset are found dead at dawn.

The following year, in the midst of a severe crisis, provoked by the India-Pakistan War[3], in the company of this same friend, I escaped the escalating situation in the North, and traveled to

South India, eventually arriving, at my insistence, to Kanchipuram, a remote village located in a South Indian jungle. I later discovered that in the eleventh century, it was in this same remote village that Mira's lineage, with the revolutionary teachings of the Bhakta Ramanuja, began.

According to legend, Ramanuja was on a pilgrimage with the disciples of Shankaracharya (the famous exponent of Advaita Vedanta). Threatened with execution for views which were considered heretical, Ramanuja's cousins informed him of a plot against his life. Escaping the danger, they secretly took him to a forest where he met a bird-catcher and his wife who promised him protection. According to the same legend, in one single night the bird catcher and his wife escorted Ramanuja, via the "astral highway" from Benares, in North East India to Kanchipuram, in South East India, thousands of miles away. Ramanuja saw, in a vision, that the bird-catcher and his wife were actually the divine pair, Lakshmi and Vishnu, and he began to teach in the very courtyard to which they had delivered him. From Ramanuja, the lineage passed (after five generations) to Ramananda, the guru of Kabir, and then to Raidas.

The ascetic Raidas was a wanderer. He travelled with a *murti* or sacred statue of Krishna, which according to the tradition, actually held or contained the *shakti* or energy of the teaching.[4] Recognizing Mira to be an archetypal *bhakta*, (destined to crystallize and express realization through one-pointed devotion), he gave this statue to her.

Mira worshipped the statue, and became completely devoted to Lord Krishna even when members of her own family and the family into which she would marry worshipped Durga. Educated to be the first Hindu Queen of the sixteenth century, Mira had been trained in poetics, music and dance. Despite this and her legendary beauty, her subsequent marriage to Prince Bhoraj of Udaipur proved to be both difficult and dangerous. She was not free to worship her chosen ishta devata nor to frequent the company of other devotees, and she scandalized her royal relatives in her efforts to do so.

Her poetry, at first, describes these problems at the court and the miraculous occurrences which saved her, after the death of her husband (and his father, a legendary warrior and king) from a series of assassination attempts. Later, her longing for absolute union with Krishna and the pain of her separation from him are its dominant themes.

Mira traveled from Rajasthan to Brindavan (in Uttar Pradesh) where the Ashta Chhap (see glossary: Vallabhacarya), under the guidance of Vallabhacarya was establishing the canonic forms of Krishna worship. At first refused entrance to the city, because she was a woman, she was later honored as the only one among the group to be capable of Radha *bhava*, actual embrace of Lord Krishna (see p. 12, note 5).

I translated these poems in Bombay with an elderly pundit, a friend of two Parsi sisters, aged and immaculate in their crumbling home by the sea. Mr. Mukerjee, a humble man, knew the tradition well and could elucidate for hours on the obscure references of the texts, as well as on their metric and melodic formulations. He patiently taught me the pronunciation of the Braja *bhasa* and the relation between the musical forms and meters of the poetry. I later studied, as a non-matriculated student at the University of Amsterdam and Delhi, with a native speaker of Braja, who was also the head of the Sanskrit Department there.

According to Vallabha, a master of poetics, (see glossary) at least three levels of 'literary' expression, *anu bhava*, *bhava bhavani*, and *kalpana* are acknowledged in the Indian system. The first refers to a text written or 'received and recorded' by one who has attained the supreme understanding and whose language is, thus, revered as a manifestation of his or her enlightened mind. The second refers to a text whose author has been "inspired" or "transported" by the sacred writings, although he or she may not be in the state which they elucidate, and the last to a text whose author has no relation to these two and thus presents an exclusively discursive or subjective (material) view.

Mira's work is considered to be of the first order, the *anu bhava*. Traditionally, in India, the translation of such texts is an anonymous act—a *seva* or service accomplished for the transformation and enlightenment of the translator and the reading (or listening) public for whom the work was intended.[5]

Independently, freely, without a publisher I tried to apply Daumal's theories of translation to Mira's *bhajans* or devotional songs. As I understood it, Mira's mode or rasa was in fact a method and means for her to address and to describe her own spiritual process . A reunion with Swami Muktananda, coincided with my arrival in Paris in 1977. A *satsang* on the outskirts of Paris revealed to me the way in which *bhakti yoga*, manifesting through and as devotional singing, can creates a matrix or base through which a disciple transforms. indeed transubstantiates his or her being, and thus the passionate emotion, the 'higher love' of the Guru-bhava and Guru puja.

The *bhavas*, or feeling modes, which describe and qualify the Braja Bhasa aesthetic, are similar to states of concentration and absorption which mark the progress of any disciple, be it he or she were a disciple of Christ or a follower of the Tibetan (see Reynolds, bibliog. no. 37 and Bhattacharya, bibliog. no.5) or any other path. The various levels of her devotion as a servant, *dasya bhava*; friend, *sakya bhava*; lover, *madhurya bhava* or parent, *vatsalya bhava*, correspond to the intensity with which a practitioner or disciple can approach and eventually unify with the "external" deity.

Nagas,
Temple, Bombay, North India

Appendix II: On word, poetry and the art of translation

Within the tradition, the male/female tensions which polarize the poetry of this saint ultimately refer to the play of energy within the microcosmic body or the tantric Shiva/Shakti, forever engaged in their blissful and inevitably painful attraction until their union is complete and the non-existence or shanti rasa is revealed.

In my translations I did not present a "personality", though it is well known that Mira was legendary in her time. Adherent of no sect, she rarely speaks of Raidas, her guru. Known to have walked the deserts of Rajasthan barefoot, accompanied by her companion, Lila, she is also said to have taught the village women dance, to have met with the great Akbar, who dressed as an ordinary man in order to hear her music, and to have Corresponded with her contemporary, Tulsidas, regarding the intrigues to which her position led.

It is said that she did not leave a body behind her, but rather united with Krishna, her beloved, in a final act of transcendence or in the actual dissolution of her body into its original elements and then into the abode of the gods or the *swarga loka*. At any rate, a Brahmanic emissary, sent to Dwarka to retrieve her, was refused entrance into her temple. She announced to the party that she would "meet them in the morning" but when dawn arrived, according to legend, all that remained inside the temple was her sari, draped across a Krishna *murti*, and her hair.

Those familiar with the Tibetan tradition, in which such phenomena have occurred, even in recent times, might ask, "What about her fingernails?"[6] Perhaps a monkey took them. We can only surmise her end and read her poetry in the work of her translators, who, no matter what our qualifications and intentions, only can approach her verse with the humble request that our resources serve it and her realization.

My challenge was to preserve intact the "transmission" which in the Braja *bhasa*, with its large flurry of Sanskrit terms (called *tatsam*) is clear. Mira celebrates her condition, through the veil of the sringara rasa, or the mode of erotic expression, specifically in its manifestation of longing or separation.

Long after I did this study, I met my teacher, the Ati yoga master, Namkhai Norbu. He inspired me to return to my own work, to heal my energy through creative expression—i.e. poetics as method. "The transmission is developed according to the potential of the individual." an older student told me. Internally, I tried to apply Mira's method to my own teacher, hoping to obtain the fruit which her poetry conceals. Arriving in America, for a retreat in 1987, I therefore felt nervous when a West Coast publisher showed interest in the translations. I feared that if this work became public my method would no longer function. And in some ways, my intuition was correct.

Although that initial publisher did not publish the work. I never again had the opportunity to practice my (secret) method of devotion so deeply and directly. After years of physically following the teacher, I had to relearn the roads of my body and seek to modify within myself the fruits of my own experience.[7]

America was like a hayfield, waiting to ignite with the karma I had left behind me. My period of a renunciate "nun" had come to an end. Though I was, at that time in my life, comfortable only with truck drivers I would meet on my peregrinations to my teacher, the simple village people who lived on the outskirts of his land in Italy, and certain old friends, Norbu Rinpoche insisted that I stay in America. He suggested that someone in America loved me. He said, "There are so many truck drivers in Italy but only one who loves you...here." And so I re-entered the world of experience, still seeking the one-pointed devotion, but now far from my teacher's external gaze.

Appendix II: On word, poetry and the art of translation

Mira was an obvious master of the 'state', her primordial condition. Her Krishna or guru, was within her. I met a young disciple in Paris who told me his teacher was a blood descendant of Mira. And why not? She wandered, she lived. She established no tradition, no sect and no convent.

Her treasure lay in her application of supreme devotion as method. The Brahmanic culture is overruled in the legend of this poet, who defied every social convention, in order to live her essence state and to liberate the conventions of her time from their confining effects on the human psyche. She brought her passion to bear on those of the highest and lowest castes of her country, without discrimination and, as a woman, fulfilled her immediate obligations without ever losing sight of the supreme one.

Perceiving the illusion of this world and yet clinging to its appearance, subject to its play and to so many of my personal shortcomings, if I now offer the Mira work, it is a simple gesture, a mudra of experience. I have been encouraged to abandon my pretense. Methods are revealed according to an individual's particular circumstance. "There are so many methods" said my teacher, three times in succession, as I described painful quarrels I had with my family.

I dedicate, once again, and finally, this work to Namkhai Norbu
and to all beings who seek realization and its poetic,
the crystallization of our body, speech and mind.
NYC 1992-1994

67

Notes to Sacred Word.

1. Knuit v.d. Veen, a Dutchman was saved from execution in a Japanese prison camp in Indonesia by realizing, in the ten minutes given to prisoners before their death, his identity with the absolute. Unable to fire the fatal shots, his would be assassins simply told him to "return home".

2. There are many illustrations, in both classical and folk art or kali-ghat of Krishna dressed as a woman or shakti, or of his disciples dressed as women, in order to worship him, or for him to be worshipped, ever more intimately.

3. I had informed the American Embassy that I was not capable of sustaining myself in the war-time environment, but they ignored my pleas to be repatriated. The Indian newspapers showed pictures of the nuclear submarines in the Bay of Bengal. At the same time the American newspapers announced, in bold headlines, "NO SUBS IN THE BAY OF BENGAL." I later found out that the bombers which flew overhead and so traumatized my consciousness, were actually American planes and this war was the first in a series of CIA military initiatives.

4. Such murti or rupa are not valued for their aesthetic qualities but rather for the power they contain and generate.. They have been effectively empowered by a master of the tradition whose iconography they manifest externally, and whose potentiality they inwardly contain.

5. Anciently, of course, texts, in the Sanskrit tradition, were said to have been directly received from the gods. The earthly scribe was therefore anonymous and the texts were said to be apurusheya or without human authorship.

6. Indian shastras (treatises) give detailed methods through which the yogi or yogini progressively dissolves the elements which comprise his or her physical body, including ether, the most subtle one. Tibetan masters

Appendix II: On word, poetry and the art of translation

Balasaraswati, Nritta (pure dance)

refer to the process whereby a practitioner, after a seven day period of concealment, manifests the *jalus* (Tib.) or rainbow body, leaving behind only traces of his or her material existence in the form of hair and fingernails. The disappearance and resurrection of Christ could be explained according to this same process.

7. Physically ill, emotionally depleted I would not have survived without the inspiration, care and protection my teacher provided at this time, a natural manifestation of his bodhicitta or compassion. I appeared at his teachings, year after year, when, rationally, my financial situation could never have supported this. "Meetings with the teacher," he once said, "do not depend on secondary factors".

Mira bhajan Sangitanjali, Vol. III. Omkarnath Thakur

APPENDIX III

THE MUSIC OF MIRABAI

As musical notation in North India was not formalized until the twentieth century, it is not possible to exactly determine the musical styles in which the *bhajans* were composed and sung. Anthologies of the sixteenth century list the poetry of the period according to the ragas which were employed and not according to the individual poets, which is a clear indication of the great importance which music had for the sensibility of the time.

According to scholars and the oral tradition itself, certain styles of composition, especially those involving group participation, used the first line or *teka* (see p.7) as a leading refrain, sung repeatedly by the group involved, while the lead singer composed new melodies for each suceeding line. The reciprocal movement of the music thus permitted the 'public' to have a direct effect on the singer's composition and fervor.

The music was preserved in *gharanas* (schools), each linked to a specific region, style and master. Ustad Ali Akbar Khan, of the Baba Allaudin Khan *gharana* (linked to the legendary musicians Haridas and Tansen, Mira's contemporaries) has composed a 'classical' style bhajan for a Mira song, in which a separate line of music is composed for each line of the verse (Khan.-Ruckert, R.1372, bilbiog. 19). Other musicians use the traditional melodies and poetic lines of the *bhajans*) to inspire musical exploration of a given raga or to further enhance their instrumental expression.

Other styles in the vocal tradition, like that of the *dhrupad* (or the *dhrupad dhamar*, specifically related to Krishna *bhakti*) may repeat, elongate or shorten various words from a single line, or improvise around a particular phrase of that line within a certain *raga* and *tala* or melodic and rhythmic pattern.

71

The poets of the *bhakti kal* used the music to intensify their poetic expression. Whereas the classical musicians subordinated the *pada* (or versification) to the powers of their musical accomplishment (*swara pradan*), the poets created a style which served as a direct support of the *pada* (*shabda pradan*) and in which the words of the song established the predominant *matra* or metric unit.

Deshi (folk) and *sastra* (classical) composition, as well as earlier liturgical motifs provided a melodic basis for the songs. In the temples of Vallabha's *Sampradaya*, the songs of the *bhakti kal* are still sung to the accompaniment of dance. Among the poets, Mira's compositions, in particuliar, have been integrated in the popular dance traditions of the North Indian regions through which she travelled as well as into the classical repertory of South Indian dance (see p. 74).

A Mira bhajan, in Indian (p.70) and Western (p.73) notation is offered as a melodic outline. The nature of Indian music does not allow a direct and complete representation. Traditionally, it is considered that the energetic content of the music is 'transmitted' orally from master to student and can not be read or learned through an intellectual process alone.

As with many aspects of traditional art, the 20th century has seen a great transformation of the above principle. The translator felt that a visual representation of a melodic mode would underline the nature of the aesthetic in which music and poetry (and dance) were indissolubly linked, and in which canons of aesthetics, as old as the *Bharatya Natya Shastra* (fourth century, B.C.) were brought into our modern world.

Mirabai moved from temple to temple, from state to state. Her songs, called (in the manuscript which is reputedly a copy of her original one), *Phutkar Padas* or Stray Devotional Songs, were spontanously composed. One can imagine, in the ambience of the temple courtyard, the intensity which

Appendix III: On the music of Mirabai

was generated by the bhajan, the devotion that filled her heart and the hearts of those with whom she sang, and why the bhajan generated hundreds and hundreds of brilliant poems in this period.

NYC 1997

RAGA MALAVAKAUSHITRA (MALKOSH)
Tala tritasla (tint)

Sthayi: Paga ghundaru bandha kara naci
Antara: Vise ka pyala ranaji ne bhejo, Mira pinbata hasi
Bapa kahe Mirabai bavarin, loga kahe kula nasi
Mira ke prabhu giradhara nagara main to teri dasi

In the above composition by Omkarnatha Thakura (see bilbiog. no. 43) the first line or *teka* of the pada is sung to the first (*sthayi*) melody and each of the succeeding lines is sung to the second (*antara*) melody. The lines are as follows *sthayi*: Silver bracelets on her feet, she dances. *antara*: The king sends poison, she drinks it with a smile. Her father says she's crazy, the people says she's ruining the clan. Mira says Ghirdhara Nagara, I'm yours.

Note on Appendix III

The principle tones in the Indian musical system are derived from animal calls, the coo-coo, lamb, goat, crane, peacock, et.al. and the names of these notes, upon which the notation is based, are derived from the names of earlier tonal divisions or scales called *jatis: sa re ga ma pa dha ni sa.*

From these seven tones or *svaras*, the scale is further divided into 22 microtones or *srutis*. These support the seven principle notes or *svara* in a series of intervals: 4 - 3 - 2 - 4 - 4 - 3 - 2. The Western system, is comprised of, instead, a twelve tone scale which only allows a semi or half tone between the seven principle notes: 2 - 2 - 1- 2 - 2 - 2 -1. In addition, in the Indian system, each of the principle notes or *svara* has a planet with which it is associated, a deity, a color, a *chakra*, a 'humour' (related to the medical system) as well as an emotional nuance or mood for each of the 22 *srutis*. The resulting composition is an integration of emotion and energy, a *raga*, whose essence can be a conscious creation, also determined by the seasons and time of day.

In addition to transcription difficulties derived from conceptual differences, the Indian third falls exactly on the ninth *sruti* whereas the Western third falls on the ninth and one half *sruti*. The Western fourth falls at the twelth and one half *sruti* whereas the Indian fourth falls exactly at the thirteenth (See Meer, bibliog. no.23). The Western third is, therefore always sharp to the Indian ear and the fourth flat, making exact transcription impossible.

A highly evolved concept of sound, wherein sound (*shabda brahma*) is the phenomena from which all others are derived is at the heart of the metaphysic, and is reflected in the most rudimentary melodic and repetitive formation.

"*Krishna ni begane baro*" Nritya (mimed dance)

DISCOGRAPHY
Amonkar, Kishori. EMC.
Anthologie de la Musique de l'Inde, Vol. 2. GREM (G 1509)
  (Alain Danielou, ed. 1 selection only)
Bedi, Dilip Chandra. *Gobardhan,* Hindustan H. 11470.
Mangeshkar, Lata. EMI ECSD 2371
Paluskar, D. V. EALP 1263.
Patwardhan, V. R. HMV-N-26000.
Padma. LLL, P. Leake and S. Taylor POPC,
lllevi32@hotmail.com
Roy, Jutika. HMV- N-16542; HMV-N-16087
Shankar, Ravi. (From the film "Mira") Premium LP, 2392-136.
Subhalakshmi, S.M.S. EMI, EALP 1297
Thakur, Omkarnath. Col. 33 - ECX 3252; COL. 33-ECX-375.
Vyasa, Narayana Rao. Twin FT. 2970.

sarangi

Ragini Todi

BIBLIOGRAPHY

1. Alston, A. J., Mirabai.*The Devotional Poems.*, Delhi:
   Motilal Barnarsidas, 1980.
2. Balbir, N., *Chants Mystiques de Mira Bai.*, Paris: Les Belles Lettres,
   1979.
3. Banerjee, P., *The Blue God.* Delhi: Lalit Kala Akademi.1981.
4. Behari, B., *Bhakta Mira.*, Bombay: Bharitya Vidya Bhavan, 1961.
5. *Bhagavata Purana.*, Delhi: Motilal Banarasidas, 1960.
6. Bhattacharya, B., *The Path of the Mystic Lover;* Rochester: Inner
   Traditions, 1993.
6. Bonnefouy, I., *On Translating Yeats,* Modern Poetry in Translation,
   London: French Issue, No. 4., Cape Golliard Press, 1972.
7. Danielou, A., *The Gods of India. Hindu Polytheism.* New York:
   Inner Traditions. 1985,
8. Das, S., *The Ashta Chhap, Lord Krishna's Eight Poet Friends.*, Delhi:
   Shri Vallabha Publications, 1985.
——*The Vena Gita. The Song of Shri Krishna's Flute.* From
   Vallabhacarya's Shri Sobodini. Unpubl. Ms.
9. Das Gupta, S. *Obscure Religious Cults.* Calcutta: Firma KLM Pvt.
   Ltd., 1976.
10. Dowman, K., *Masters of Mahamudra,* Albany: State Univ. of
    New York Press., 1985.
11. *Daumal, R.,* Bharata, Paris: Gallimard, 1970.
——L.L.-Levi(transl.) *Rasa: Essays on Indian Aesthetics and
   Selected Sanskrit Studies.*, New York: New Directions, 1982.
12. Esnoul, A.M., *Ramanuja et la mystique Vishnouvite.*, Paris: Seuil,
    1964.
13. Friedman, H., Virah Bhakti. *The Early History of Krsna Devotion
    in South India,* Delhi: Oxford University Press, 1983.
14. Gnoli, R., *The Aesthetic Experience according to Abhinavagupta,*
    Rome: Institute. Italiano, 1956.
15. Goetz, H., *Mira Bai,* Bombay: Bharitya Vidya Bhavan, 1966.
16. Hawley, J.S., *At Play with Krishna: Pilgrimage Dramas from
    Brindavan.*, Princeton: Princeton University Press, 1981.

77

17. Hein, N., *The Miracle Plays of Matura*. New Haven: Yale Univ. Pr.,1942,
18. Isacco, E.& A. L. Dallapiccola, Krishna. *The Divine Lover.* Boston: David R. Godine.1982.
19. Khan, A. A.-G. Ruckert(ed), *The Classical Music of North India.* St. Louis: Eastbay Books, 1991.
20. Machwe, P., *Kabir.* Delhi: Sahitya Akademi, 1968.
21. Mahesh, M.,*The Historical Development of Medieval Hindi Prosody,* Bhagalpur: Bhagalpur University, 1964.
22. Mcdaniel, J., *The Madness of the Saints.* Chicago: Univ. of Chicago. Pr., 1989.
23. Meer, v.d.-J.Bor, De Reop van de Kokila. *S'gravenhage.* Nijhoff, 1982.
24. *Mira Bhajan Mala.,* Mathura: Shyam Kasi Press, ND.
25. *Miran Buhatpadavali,* Jodhpur: Rajasthan Dr. Res. Inst., 1968.
26. Morrison, D., *A Glossary of Sanskrit: From the Spiritual Tradition of India,* npl, Nilgiri Press, 1970
27. Muktananda, T*he Way of a Siddha. Conversations.* So. Fallsburg: SYDA, 1979.
——*The Nectar of Chanting.* So. Fallsburg: SYDA, 1979
28. Nandas-R.S. Mc Gregor (transl.), *The Round Dance of Krishna and Uddev's Message,* London: Luzac and Company,1973.
29. Narada, *The Bhakti Sutras.,* Allahabad: Sudhinora Natha Vasa, 1911.
30. Nilsson, U., *Mira-Bai.,* New Delhi: Sahitya Akademi, 1969.
31. Neog, M., *The Contribution of the Sankaradev Movement to the Culture and Civilisation of India.* Guwahati: Sankaradeva Adhyayana Kshetra. 1988.
32. Norbu, N. J. Reynolds (transl.), *The Cycle of Day and Night,* Barrytown: Station Hill Press, 1988.
—— *A. Clemente (ed.) & J. Shane(transl.) Dzog-Chen. The Self-Perfected State.* London: Arkana. 1989.
33. Ragavan, V., *The Indian Cultural Heritage,* Delhi: Motilal Banarsidas, 1964.
34. Ram Avatar Vir, *Theory of Indian Music.* New Delhi: Pankaj Publications, 1980.

Bibliography

35. Ramana Maharshi, *Maharshi's Gospel,* Tiruvanimali: Sri Ramanasramam, 1969.
36. Ramanujan, A.K., *Speaking of Siva,* Middlesex: Penguin Books, 1973.
37. Reynolds, J., Garab Dorje. *The Golden Letters.* Ithaca: Snow Lion Pr.,1996.
38. Scripps, L. & T. Viswanarthan. Balasaraswati. *A Tribute to the Artist and Her Art.* NP. Balasaraswati School of Music and Dance. 1986.
39. Schelling, A., *For Love of the Dark One. Songs of Mira Bai.* Boston: Shambhala, 1993.
40. Shantsheela, S. *Contribution of Saints and Seers to the Music of India,* Vol. 1. New Delhi: Kanislaka Publ., 1996.
41. Siegel, L., *Sacred and Profane Dimensions of Love in Indian Tradition as Exemplified in the Gita Govinda.* Delhi: Oxford Univ. Pr., 1990. 37.
42. Singh, G, *Le Canzoni di Mira.* Urbino. Quattro Venti. 1987
43. Stoller Miller, B., Jayadeva. *The Gita Govinda.* New York City: Columbia Univ. Pr., 1978
44. Tharu, S. & K.K. Lalita, *Women Writings in India.* New York City: Feminist Press. 1991.
45. Thakura, O. *Sangitangali,*vol.3 Banares: np.1955.
46. Varma, D., *Braj: dialecte de Mathura.,* Paris: Adrien Maisonneuve, 1935.
47. Vaidya, C. and B.N. Shastri. *Shri Vallabhacarya: His Teachings.* Delhi: 1984.- Transl. from the German.
48. Walker, B., *An Encyclopedic Survey of Hinduism and the Hindu World.* 2 vols. New Delhi: Motilal Banarsidas. 1983.
49. Woodroffe, J. *The Serpent Power.,* Madras: Ganesh Press, 1974.

GLOSSARY

GODS & GODDESSES

Krishna: From the Sanskrit root *krs* meaning 'to drag, (or to draw into one's power), to give 'pain', signifying the "age of pain", the *kali yuga*. "Should the name of Krishna but once come across the mind of the devotee, it takes away, devours, eliminates the suffering inherent in this age of conflict." The essence and importance of Lord Krishna is beyond estimation in the art, literature, spiritual science and iconography of India. Emerging from an ancient tradition nascent in the *Rig Veda* (where Krishna was considered one of the twelve *adityas* or sun gods), developed in the *Chandoyoga Upanisad*, the *Mahabharata* (where Krishna appears in human form in the fourteenth chapter, the Bhagavad Gita) and the Bhagavata Purana (circa. ninth century. A.D.). In the period which followed the evolution of Sanskrit into Prakrit (or natural) languages, Krishna flourished as a principle figure of devotion, transformation and representation. Together with his consort Radha (see below), his love dalliance catalyzed the emerging consciousness erotic and divine of medieval North India. The questions of temporality and eternity were dealt with more directly than ever before in the popular tradition of India and both esoteric and exoteric sciences of love underwent a radical transformation (See Siegel, bibliog.no.41).

Radha: From the Sanskrit root *radh*, meaning to submit, to propitiate, to gratify, and radha, literally, gift or favor. Principal consort of Lord Krishna, in the Indian traditional science, she is regarded as an emanation or incarnation of Lakshmi, Shri, the consort of Vishnu (see below) and in the *Rig Veda*, goddess of the 'creative' waters. Historically, she was the favored among the *gopi*

Glossary

friends of the young god, and was his partner in the raslila. Esoterically she is the symbol of deliverance through devotion, but on an absolute plane she is the equal of Krishna. As a popular figure, Radha concentrated the energies of the reemergent matriarchy, returning popular worship to the female deity, and the 'beautiful and brutal' aspects of the goddess figure (Siegel, ibid.).

Shakti: Technically, in the *tantric* texts, the *shakti* or female energy is the manifestation and movement itself of this world. Shakti resides in the human body, particularly in the *kundalini* and *chakras* (see below) but is present in all animate and inanimate creation. She is considered the active component of the absolute bliss of Shiva. She is the seed of liberation—the object of worship in the Indian tantra.

Shiva: Viewed in the trinity of the Hindu pantheon, Shiva is the god of destruction, whereas Brahma is the god of creation and Vishnu of preservation. In the absolute sense, he is *para* Shiva, immobile, unchanging and absolute, whose manifestation *shakti* gives the animate universe its energy. His forms are ascetic, erotic and aesthetic and as such he the lord of yoga, of the art of love and, in his form, Shiva Nataraja, the lord of dance.

Vasudeva: An epithet for Krishna, meaning, lit. in Sanskrit, *vasu*, of Vishnu, and *deva*, god or light.

Vishnu: The lord of preservation (see above), he has ten principle '*avatars*' or forms, the first of which is a fish, the last of which is Kalki, the 'savior' of mankind, who is yet to come. Each of the forms corresponds to the principle *yugas* or cosmic time periods. Krishna and Buddha are considered to be the avatars of the *kali yuga*, the fourth, in which we live. Krishna alone, however, is worshipped as a 'total' incarnation, a *purnavatara* by Vaishnavite sects. "Limitless his qualities, his actions, the manifestations of his power are endless. Having manifested the world, he enters it again as its guide. Having created it, he entered it"(*Tattiriya Upanishad*).

HISTORICAL FIGURES

Chandidasa: A poet-saint of the sixteenth century in West Bengal, Chandidasa lived in the courtyard of the Bashuli Devi temple. He scandalized his Brahmanic peers by marrying Rami, a washerwoman (others assert that her name was Rukajini and that she too was a poet). His principle work, *Ragatmika-Pada, Songs of Passionate Devotion* was written in medieval Bengali. "There are two currents in the lake of love, realized only by the *rasika* (the knower of the *rasa*)". "The feet of the washerwoman are the highest truth." "The love of the washerwoman is like tested gold says Badu Chandidasa"

Chaitanya: (1485-1553) Saint and lover, Chaitanya spent much of his life in mystic trance, absorbed in a devotional *bhava* which was beyond both speech and ritual. He worshipped the Krishna image at the Jagannath temple in Puri but was considered by some to be, himself, Krishna, or Radha, or both (see the *Chaitanya Bhagavata* or the *Chaitanya Caritamrta*). For the Vaishnavite he exemplified the perfection of devotion. Ecstatic with love, he is said to have disappeared before his disciples without any manifestation of death.

Jayadeva: Brilliant Sanskrit poet of the twelveth century, court poet to the last Sena king, Jayadeva, was an ascetic who, it is said, through his marriage to Padmavati achieved his great work *The Gita Govinda*. Perfectly merging the threads of the human and divine in love, this poem is considered to be a masterpiece of the Vaishnavite tradition and a perfect manifestation of Lord Krishna's grace. Some sources say that Mirabai wrote a commentary on the *Gita Govinda* (and on the *Rag Govind*) but these manuscripts are not traceable. "His musical skill, his meditation on Vishnu, his vision of reality in the erotic mood, his graceful play in these poems, all show that master-poet Jayadeva's soul is in perfect tune with Krishna" (Transl. B. Stoller-Miller, bibliog.no.43)

Glossary

Kabir: (1440-1518) A student of Ramananda, Kabir, a married householder yogi, was a weaver by day and master by night. He tricked Ramananda (see below) into giving him the lineage initiation (Kabir was, technically, not an 'official' Hindu, having been found and raised, as an orphan, by Moslem parents) and went on to become its most popular exponent in the local language *Naga Kari*. His *padas* were powerful agents of reconciliation between Hindus and Moslems in North India, especially in Kashi or Benares, where he lived. A *nirguna* (see preface) guru, Kabir was also one of the great religious critics of his times. "If you don't cross over alive, how can you cross when you're dead?" Kabir says "seekers listen, wherever you are is the entry point." (Bijak, transl. L.Hess & Singh)

Raidas: This ascetic master, also referred to as Ravidas, received initiation from Ramananda, and is reputed to have been Mira's teacher or spiritual mentor. He wandered anonymously in North West India and is said to have initiated Mira spontaneously through a divinely empowered statue of Krishna (see cover).

Ramananda: (1400-1470) A revolutionary teacher, Ramananda sowed the seeds of Ramanuja's lineage (see below) in North India principally through his twelve disciples, the most well-known of whom are Raidas and Kabir. He taught a direct path to the divine. Accessible to disciples regardless of culture and caste, the absolute dwelt equally in all beings and was realized through incessant recollection. The principle means of this recollection were *bhajan, kirtan* and *satsang* (see glossary).

Ramanuja: In the eleventh century, in the tradition of the Alvars, the twelve devotees of Tamil Nadu, Ramanuja defied, then sought to modify and to transform the teaching of Shankaracharya. His *Shri Bhasya*, (a Vedic commentary in Sanskrit) affirmed a devotional relation (visisthadvaita) between disciple and deity. Devotion or bhakti supplanted established paths, encouraging its adepts to use emotion and sensation to recognize and to awaken their own divinity.

Shankaracharya: (788-820) This Brahmanic scholar, teacher and renunciate ("a humble pupil of Gaudapadacharya") reformed, and according to some, saved the Hindu world with his immaculate teaching of the *Veda*, and his view of the non-dual (*dvaita*, dual, *advaita*, non-dual) illusory world where, according to the same teaching, realization, is possible. The distinction between the supreme and individual soul was considered to be 'unreal', and the methods used were based on renunciation and merit. Shankaracharya's *advaitic* Vedanta was an ascetic interpretation of the Indian metaphysic and depended on the Brahmanic injunctions. His principle works are the Ananda and Saundarya Lahari .

Tansen: (1532-date unknown) A student of the musician hermit of Gwalior, Haridas, Mian Tansen was invited to be and became the principle musician at the court of Akbar. Reputed to have had legendary control over *raga* and *tala*, his lineage is still alive today. One of its greatest living exponents is the daughter of Allaudin Khan, Shrimati Annupurnadevi.

Tulsidas: (l534-1623) Devoted to lord Rama, the seventh incarnation of Vishnu, lover of Hanuman, the monkey king and servant, Tulsidas wrote the *Ramachitamanas*, the first great devotional work in what is now the popular language of North India, Hindi. The text *The Lake of the Acts of Rama* is an innovative retelling of Valmiki's epic, Ramayana, which was written in Sanskrit. Tulsidas also wrote the *Hanuman Chalisa*, a fourty line prayer still sung by disciples who through this song seek Lord Hanuman's presence, love and assistance.

Vallabhacarya: (l48l-1553) Master of Braja and founder of the Ashta Chap, the eight seals or 'brothers of lord Krishna', Vallabha united in himself the teaching of the *Veda*, *Upanisad* and *Purana* and established, with his son, Vithalnath, the pushita marg, the path of grace. Leaving behind innumerable works on Radha and Krishna, devotion and aesthetics, the Ashta Chap included some of the finest poets of the day, Surdas, Namdev et.al. "Krishna's *lilas* effortlessly enlighten anyone who comes into contact with them. What is there to be liberated from?" (Shri Sobodhini, Vallabha's study of the Shrimad Bhagavat).

Vidyapati: (1368-1476) A court poet and Brahmin, friend to the heir apparent of the throne of Kirti Simha, Vidyapati wrote his hymns to Krishna in Maithili. His work, including the Bhuparikrama. achieved a widespread following and was adapted to the Vaishnava tradition by Chaitanya himself: "Listen, O precious lady, in prolonged thirst, one drinks water profusely."

TERMS

Atman: From the Pali *atta*, of "the nature of pure consciousness." According to Daumal: "In the *Veda* it is still related to the image of 'vital breath'. *Atman*, self, is that with which the being identifies when saying, 'I'. This can be the social and exterior personality of the body, feelings and thoughts—all this illusion. For he who made himself, the *atman* is the 'master of the chariot', described in the Katha Upanishad, or the divine personage, or the absolute being" (*Rasa*, see Glossary/Terms).

Bhava: From the Sanskrit root *bha*, feelings which qualify principle emotions, literally 'existences'. "The savour (*rasa*) is differentiated according to states or modes of existence (*bhavas*) of which it is the 'supernatural' and disinterested perception" (Daumal). In popular language: intense feeling generated by the aesthetic experience of uniting subjective emotion with objective experience. For the Vaishnavite *bhava* is a means to as well as a gift from the deity .

Brahman: From the Sanskrit root *brh*, to grow, defined by Danielou as the "divine immensity", the source of the universe in the Upanisads, the sole reality (*aham brahmasmi* I am Brahman) in Advaita Vedanta. In the Hindu trinity (see above) Brahma is the god of creation. The Hindu caste system differentiates at least 4 distinct groups, of which the Brahmins are the sacerdotal and absolutely reserved class. "Bliss (*ananda*) is to be known as Brahman, and from bliss proceeds all objects and through bliss they live and in bliss they return and merge"(*Taithiriyopanishad*).

Caryapada: Songs of realization (*circa*. 8th-12th century), the *Caryapada* were written in *Aparabramsa* by the *siddha* and *sahajiya* poets of Northeastern India, (*pada*, lit. in Sanskrit, 'foot', the second and fourth line of a four line stanza.)

Chakra: Lit. in Sanskrit, wheel, there are, in the Hindu tantra seven principle ones, whose function is related to specific energies and spiritual attainments. "This family woman (*kundalini*) entering the royal road (*susumna*) taking rest at intervals in the sacred places (*cakras*) embraces the supreme husband (*para-shiva*) and makes nectar to flow from the sahasrara" *Cintamati Satva*, Shankaracarya (See p.12 note no.4 & illustration p.51).

Darshan: From the Sanskrit *darshana*, to see, and also to be seen , a meeting with a spiritual master, "seeing or being in the presence of a revered person, sacred image or sacred place."

Devanagari: The name of the alphabet in which Sanskrit (and some of the subsequent prakrit or spoken languages of North India) is written. The alphabet has from 33 to 36 consonants and from 12 to 16 vowels, depending on the system of classification. In the tantric tradition, the letters are considered to be forms of shakti and to directly manifest the goddess', or *kundalini* energy. They are located as well, in the subtle body of the human being spread around the *chakras* like petals on a flower (see p.51).

Guru: In Sanskrit *gu*, heavy and *ru*, light, also mountain, are among the many qualifications of this word. A spiritual teacher, a being capable of transmitting spiritual, or other, knowledge. In the tradition, the guru embodies divine power. He or she is a liberated being, a *jivamukti* who, through initiation, awakens the disciple's inner state, The guru is considered indispensable for *tantric* practice.

Kalighat: A school of art or folk art generally from Bengal in North East India

Kundalini: The 'serpent power' at the base of the spine, seat of the concealed female energy in the human body. "Upon the bursting (unfolding) of the supreme bindu arose unmanifest sound. It assumed the form of kundalini in living bodies and manifested itself in prose and verse by the aid of the letters of the alphabet." Sarada.- Woodroffe, bibliog.no. 49).

Kriya, carya & yoga tantra: "According to the Nyingmapa or 'ancient school', (of Tibetan Buddhism) *kriya, carya* and *yoga tantra* are called the external *tantras*, because the practices involved are principally based on purification, the preparation for wisdom." (Clemente-Shane). In the *kriya tantra*, emphasis is on external ritual, and the deity is approached as if one were a servant. In the *carya tantra*, the deity is approached through external ritual and internal mediation and is considered to be a friend. In the *yoga tantra*, the *yoga* is a means of unification, "beginning with supplication, the practitioner enters into mystical union with the deity" (Reynolds). In the Tibetan tradition the *tantra* is considered to be of non-human origin. Its visualization, in the center of which is the deity, is called a *mandala*. In both the Hindu and Buddhist tradition, the *tantric* practice offers direct means of realization, often involving radical departure from the orthodoxy.

Mantra: From the Sanskrit root, *man* meaning mind and *tra* to protect. *Mantra*, a subtle sound form of the *devi* or *deva*, is considered to be the mind's ultimate protection. Mantras are Sanskrit words or syllables. They express the quiescence of various energies whether or not the mantra has conceptual content. From the view of fruition (in the Tibetan tradition) the practitioner should recognize all sound as mantra, all appearance as the deity and all thoughts as wisdom.)

Pandit: From the Sanskrit root, *pan*, meaning learned, or expert, an honorific title, implying mastery. *Pandit*, in the medieval period, indicated a knowledge of Sanskrit.

Rasa: From the Sanskrit root ras lit. taste, or savor, in the system of aesthetics, also fluids, especially sexual, internal fluids in the tantric system. Abhinavagupta (see Intro., note 3) gives special place to the term, because *rasa* is capable of liberating, through aesthetic experience, the ego from *samsara*. The *rasas* are technically divided into at least eight and sometimes nine or ten categories: *sringara* (love), *karuna* (compassion), *hamsa* (humor) et.al.(See Daumal, bibliog.no. 11). "The savor belongs neither to the poet nor to the auditor, neither to the actor nor to the spectator, but it unites them in a single moment of consciousness" (*Sahityadarpana*). The *Raslila* (from the Sanskrit root *lila* to play) is the circle dance which Krishna enacts with Radha, his consort. The gopis dance around the divine pair each one believing that Krishna is her partner in the dance. Esoterically, the *raslila* is an integration of consciousness with the qualifications of the human psyche animated in the aesthetic theory of *rasa*.

Sadhana: From the Sanskrit root *sadh*, to aim, to direct, to attain. In the tradition, spiritual practice leading to realization.

Sarangi: Literally, the instrument of one hundred colors, the *sarangi* is a bowed-harp. Three principle gut strings are bowed and forty or more metal strings are tuned to the principal raga or composition.

Satsang: From the Sanskrit root *sat*, being, and *sang*, association or gathering. A meeting with one's spiritual companions or teacher, opportunity for collective practice, through contemplation, ritual, music, dance et.al.

Siddha: From the Sanskrit root *sid* meaning adept, also, to be perfect. One who possesses the eight supernatural powers or who has gone beyond them. The *mahasiddhas* were highly initiated beings who taught in forms not usually associated with spiritual heritage (they were wanderers, prostitutes, musicians, but also kings, queens and servants). They are said to have received initiation through visionary means, and through application and devotion to have realized the alchemical transformations they were taught.

Glossary

Tantra: From the Sanskrit root tan, literally continuity, or thread. In the Indian tradition the term indicates a body of work which was heretic to the Brahmanic heritage and in which the female goddess was the central point of instruction and offering. In the Tibetan tradition, (see above) the tantra is not contained in the oral teaching (of a master like Shakymuni Buddha) but said to reside in the energy of the elements themselves, in the subtle dimension of sound and light, to be transmitted to our human world through beings who reside in that dimension.

Vaishnaiva: The school of Krishna devotion which arose in South India after the eleventh century, and came to flowering in North India in the fifteenth and sixteenth century. The Vaishnavas worshipped Krishna as the eighth manifestation of Vishnu and as the absolute being. In this system the deity was perceived as human in his characteristics and divine in his capacities.

Vedanta: From the Sanskrit root vid meaning knowledge, the body of knowledge derived from the four *Veda*. The *Vedas* were essentially ritual and social codes of conduct. The *Samhita, Brahmana* and *Avanyate*, considered adjuncts to them, were collections of hymns, spells and secret ('forest') teaching and the *Upanishad* were their "knowledge" or "end" part ("That which resolves completely, to the 'end'", Shankaracharya). The goal of life, according to these texts, is realization of Brahman. The *Vedanta* are commentaries on the body of knowledge, delineated and preserved in the four *Veda*.

BOOKS
Poems, 1972
The Water-Mirror, 1982
Departure, 1983
Amiata, 1984
Concerto, 1988
Extinction, 1990
Guru Punk, 1992
The Tower, 1993
The Highway Queen, 1994
The House Lamps Have Been Built but ..., 1996
Chorma, 2000
Makar/A kar'MA, 2002
The Book L, 2010
Crazy Louise, 2013

TRANSLATIONS
Daumal, R., *RASA, Essays on Indian Aesthetics and Selected Sanskrit Studies*, 1982
Michaux, H., *Vers La Complétude*, 1984

LIBRETTOS
The Kama Sutra, 1994

RECORDINGS
Kinnari. Sarangi, Kinnara and Voice, 1984
Padma. Sarangi, flute and voice, 1988
Kyerang, Music for Meditation, 1992
Sweet on My Lips

POETRY RECORDINGS
Kunst is Die Liefde in Elke Daad, with
Simon Vinkenoog, 1985
Oasis, with Joel O'Brien. 1992
Neptune, 1997
City of Delerium, 2010

About the Author

Louise Landes Levi was born in New York City and now lives in Italy. She lived in North India for nearly three years and studied Indian music, primarily in Bombay. Her travels led her to the principal sites of Mira's hagiography and to a native speaker of Mira's 16th century Braja Bhasa. Ms. Levi publishes, performs and records her work in Europe and the USA. She has taught at Naropa Institute and been a guest lecturer at the Manhattan School of Music, Bard College, and the Jivamukti Yoga Center.

the love poems of Mirabai

Made in the USA
Columbia, SC
27 July 2022

64116930R00069